PATRIC

Overcoming Stress

A CHRISTIAN PERSPECTIVE

A heart at peace gives life to the body.
Proverbs 14:30

VERITAS

First published 1989 by
All Hallows

This edition published 1989 by
Veritas Publications
7/8 Lower Abbey Street
Dublin 1

ISBN 1 85390 110 5

Cover design by Lucia Happel
Typesetting by Printset & Design Ltd, Dublin
Printed in the Republic of Ireland by Paceprint Ltd, Dublin

A PERSONAL EXPERIENCE OF STRESS

A few years ago I headed off with two colleagues to conduct a parish mission. Normally I would have been enthusiastic. But not on this occasion. Instead, I dreaded the prospect of meeting strangers and dealing with their many problems. On our very first morning in the parish I got off to a bad start. I became quite abrasive with a woman who had annoyed me. Afterwards I felt rotten. Why had I lost my self-control in such an unreasonable and hurtful way? I began to realise that I did not feel well. I was tense, up-tight and reluctant to face any kind of pressure. So I came to a difficult and embarrassing decision. It would be better for the team, the parishioners and myself if I withdrew from the mission.

For the next few months I felt miserable. I could not sleep well. I always felt tired. I got many dull headaches. They could last for days and were unaffected by aspirin. I felt anxious and apprehensive all the time. On one or two occasions I felt a real sense of panic. Over and over again, I asked myself the question, 'What is happening to me?' I did not really know, but I was determined to find out.

Then as a result of a lot of reading and reflection, I came to recognise that I was suffering from 'burn-out'. It is a form of emotional exhaustion which is brought on by unhealthy levels of unrelieved stress. Some of it had been triggered by outer environmental factors such as the demanding nature of my work. Still more had been occasioned by inward psychological causes such as an exaggerated fear of failure. But there was reason for hope. I began to realise that the pain of stress is nature's red light. It was warning me that the way I was living was not working. It was inviting me to make the necessary psychological and environmental changes that would help me to recover. Over a period of time I came to terms with these issues. I learned to relax and so regained my sense of personal well-being and peace.

Carl Jung once wrote: 'There is no growth in consciousness without pain'. Looking back, I can see how the experience of stress was for me a blessing in disguise. It forced me to take stock in many ways. As a result I grew in self-awareness and made a number of practical changes in my lifestyle. St Paul says that we are comforted in our troubles 'so that we may be able to comfort those who are in any trouble, with the comfort with which we ourselves are comforted' (*2 Cor 1:4*). Hence this booklet. It is written in the belief that if you or someone you care about suffers from unhealthy levels of stress it can and should be overcome. Stress is an invitation to change and to grow.

THE NATURE OF STRESS

Stress is nervous tension. We have already noted that it can be caused by environmental and psychological factors. These can lead to either **acute** or **chronic** stress. Stress is acute when it is sharp but short-lived. By and large it does not do us much harm. Indeed it may be helpful in the sense that it adds an extra edge to our performance, e.g. when running in a race or acting in a play. Stress becomes chronic when it persists in an unrelieved way. Combining these points we can look at a number of examples.

1. **Acute environmental stress** could be experienced when a person has to move quickly to catch a valuable vase as it falls from the mantlepiece.

2. **Chronic environmental stress** could be experienced by a person who has to work in an extremely noisy factory.

3. **Acute psychological stress** could occur as a result of hicupping during an important speech.

4. **Chronic psychological stress** could be the outcome of having to cope with a bad marriage to an alcoholic partner.

So stress can be triggered by any number of things. But in the last analysis it is a largely subjective event. **It depends on the person's reaction — not on an outside event.** That said, the experience of stress is always the same. Nature has equipped us to cope with perceived dangers. In an emergency situation the body goes on alert. Automatically the brain triggers a sequence of physiological changes. Hormones in the form of adrenalin are produced. Digestion slows. Blood pressure rises. Perspiration increases. The eyeballs retract, while the pupils and also the nostrils and bronchi dilate. Sugars and fats are secreted to provide the body with extra energy. Muscles grow tense, ready for 'flight or fight'. This primitive reaction was very helpful when our ancestors had to cope with life and death situations. After all, they had to face regular attacks from either animals or enemies. It gave them the extra strength they needed to take appropriate action. As a result of their vigorous efforts their emergency supplies of energy were used up, and so they returned to a state of relaxation.

While the challenges and demands of modern life are many, they are rarely life-threatening. Even when they are, e.g. having to brake suddenly to avoid an accident, we do not really need the extra energy the body supplies. All we do is to move one foot to jam on the brakes. When the emergency has passed we remain keyed-up because we have not used up our bonus energy. The same is true when we are faced by the lesser crises of everyday life, such as deadlines to meet, appointments to keep, bills to be paid, etc. As a result our 'flight or fight' response is activated over and over again in an inappropriate way. Stress levels go up so that acute stress becomes chronic. If it remains unrelieved, it can have a harmful physical, psychological and spiritual effect.

TRANSITIONAL CRISES AND STRESS

While we can experience stress at any time in our lives, it is more likely to occur during times of painful change. Cardinal Newman once observed that 'to live is to change'. This is biologically true. Apparently every cell within us is replaced every seven years or so. We change psychologically and spiritually also. This is particularly true during times of personal crisis. These are *the* turning points for better or for worse in our lives.

There are two main forces of crisis, predictable and unpredictable. Psychologists say that **predictable crises** occur regularly throughout our lives. They precede the main developmental phases, e.g. before the onset of early, middle and late adulthood. Daniel Levinson says that these transitions occur between the ages of 17 and 22, 40 and 45, and 60 and 65 approximately. He also indicates that we can expect lesser transitions between the ages of 28 and 33, and again between 50 and 55 approximately. The purpose of these crises is to urge us to tackle some specific developmental task. By doing so we grow into a new depth of maturity. **Unpredictable crises** occur when the 'Slings and arrows of outrageous fortune' come our way. We may be pitched into a period of turmoil and soul-searching by the death of a close relative, the news that we have cancer or by the loss of our job. Often a predictable crisis will occur at the same time as one or two unpredictable ones. Transitional crises of either kind have a threefold structure.

a) Onset of restlessness

A woman could face a predictable crisis with the onset of the menopause. At the same time she might have to cope with the fact that her husband has lost his job and that her unmarried daughter has become pregnant. Like countless other people she enters a time of painful transition. She may feel that she is losing control over her life. She lives in a sort of emotional 'no man's land' where things happen to her. She feels like a victim. Troubling feelings seep up from the unconscious levels of her experience, e.g. anxiety, fear, insecurity, guilt, confusion, mild depression, etc. She enters a stressful period because her life seems subject to anonymous threats that evoke her 'flight or fight' response on a daily if not an hourly basis.

b) Darkness and exploration

Times of crisis for a woman like this are often times of disillusionment. The way she looked at herself and her priorities is challenged. Beliefs and values that sustained her in the past seem strangely inadequate now. Not surprisingly, she loses her inner sense of joy and peace. Instead she feels agitated and restless. As the scaffolding that supported her self-image is removed, there can be a real sense of loss and grief. Her sense of hurt may give rise to a feeling of anger with herself, with others, and perhaps with God. Like many others she may try to repress these feelings. As a result they could turn inwards to attack her, thereby making her feel more insecure, inadequate and helpless. This kind of dynamic can lead to a lot of strain and tension.

During a crisis all kinds of questions surface:

— Why is my self-esteem so low?
— Why is it that I am always trying to please others and to win their approval?
— Why am I a perfectionist and so hard on myself when I fail?
— Why am I driven by a sense of obligation, rather than being motivated by personal conviction?
— Why am I always in a hurry with too many things to do?
— Why can't I ever say 'no' to people?
— Why do I have so little time for friends or leisure activities?
— How come I cannot stand up for myself and assert my dignity and rights when I am being badly treated?
— When there is an argument or conflict of any kind, why do I need peace at any price?

These and many other questions can arise during a time of transition. They are important. They may be pointing to the largely unconscious attitudes and assumptions that have been causing so much stress in our lives.

c) Resolution and restabilisation

As our defence mechanisms begin to crumble during a time of crisis, we may get in touch with basic questions to do with our identity and values. As we answer them we begin to let go of our former assumptions and attitudes. As we do so, we embrace more appropriate and realistic ones. For example, the menopausal woman with family problems may discover that all her life she has been too pre-occupied with public opinion. As she becomes more inner directed her sense of security increases while her feelings of stress grow weaker.

5

THE SIGNS AND EFFECTS OF UNRELIEVED STRESS

a) The signs of physical stress

When a person is suffering from physical tension it can have the following knock-on effects on different parts of the body.

1. CARDIOVASCULAR: palpitations, racing heart, dizziness, faintness, fear of losing consciousness, blushing, migraine headaches, cold hands and feet.

2. RESPIRATORY: unable to get enough air, hyperventilation, i.e. fast, shallow breathing, chest constriction.

3. MUSCULAR: tension headaches, shaking, severe weakness, restless body or legs, jaw grinding.

4. GASTROINTESTINAL: butterflies in the stomach, nausea, vomiting, wind, flatulence, burping, abdominal pain, cramps and diarrhoea.

b) The effects of chronic physical stress

1. It can directly cause such problems as high blood-pressure. This in turn can lead to kidney disease, strokes and heart failure. All of these conditions can be life-threatening. Stress can also cause ulcers, asthmatic problems, build-up of cholesterol, etc.

2. It can aggravate conditions such as backache, arthritis, multiple sclerosis, allergies, skin conditions, hyperthyroidism, etc.

3. It weakens the body's defence system. As a result it is more vulnerable to infections of all kinds, e.g. the common cold, flu and even cancer.

It is estimated by the medical profession that at least sixty per cent and possibly eighty per cent of all sickness is stress-related.

c) The signs of psychological stress

There are many signs of psychological tension, e.g. feeling anxious, social fears, fear of heights, or darkness, or being alone, low self-esteem, sleeping difficulties, etc.

d) The effects of chronic psychological stress

1. The person may suffer from panic attacks, a feeling of inner terror.

2. The person finds it hard to cope with any pressure. He suffers from outbursts of impatience, anger and hostility.

3. His concentration slips, he makes mistakes more often, e.g. locking the keys in the car... while the engine is running! Mental blocks are common, e.g. forgetting appointments and names. Sleep is disturbed by many dreams and nightmares. Afterwards the person gets up feeling tired and tense.

4. The victim of stress may try to escape the pain of his condition in ways that reinforce the problem.

   - Eating has been called 'nature's tranquilliser'. If a stressful person eats too much he will feel guilty as his weight goes up. As a result his self-esteem will drop while his stress levels rise.

   - Many people suffering from stress feel thirsty and tired, so they drink endless cups of coffee and tea. Both tannin and caffeine are stimulants that increase stress.

   - Many people try to deaden the pain of stress with alcohol. It is true that it may relax a person for a time. It may make it easier to get off to sleep, but the sleep will be shallow as a result. And so the drinker will get up feeling tired and ill-equipped to meet the challenges of a new day. In some cases alcohol abuse can lead to addictions, accidents, domestic strife, loss of job etc. — all of which are stressful.

- In an emergency situation tranquillisers and sleeping pills can be helpful if they are prescribed for a short period, i.e. six weeks at most. But if the stressful person comes to rely on them, they become part of the problem instead of being part of the solution.

- It is commonly thought that smoking has a tranquillising effect. Perhaps the oral activity, reminiscent of being breast-fed is reassuring, but nicotine is a stimulant and so increases stress. Many of the illnesses that come from smoking do not do much for stress levels either.

5. Chronic stress can lead to all kinds of physical problems, e.g. irregular periods in women and impotence in men. These difficulties reinforce stressful feelings.

6. Unrelieved stress can lead to 'burn-out' or 'compassion fatigue' as it has sometimes been called. Jerry Edelwich has described it as a 'Progressive loss of idealism, energy and purpose experienced by people in the helping professions'. That would include individuals such as social workers, counsellors, therapists, spiritual directors, doctors, nurses, chaplains and clergymen of all kinds. In my experience 'burn-out' can afflict anyone, e.g. housewives, journalists, broadcasters, police men and women, dentists, pilots, etc. According to psychologists 'burn-out' has three degress of severity.

The first degree of 'burn-out' is common. Warning signs include an inability to shake off a lingering cold, frequent headaches and sleeplessness. That said, the person continues to work without much sign of trouble.

The second degree of 'burn-out' occurs when the symptoms of the first stage consolidate and get worse. The person suffers from fatigue, prolonged headaches, angry outbursts, irritability and impatience. He worries too much about problems and may treat other people badly. For example, a teacher who is normally polite and considerate ends up shouting at his colleagues. At this stage job performance begins to suffer. The person becomes more detached and impersonal while saying

'It's not that I don't want to help, I can't'. Paradoxically, instead of taking things easier, typical sufferers take on extra work. But instead of achieving more, they actually accomplish less while reinforcing their stress.

The third degree of 'burn-out' occurs when the symptoms become chronic. At this stage the person is unable to function normally. Physical sickness is common, e.g. heart-attacks, high blood-pressure, etc. Psychological difficulties are to be expected, e.g. severe depression, feelings of extreme loneliness and isolation, together with suicidal inclinations.

e) The spiritual effects of chronic stress

The experience of 'burn-out' can be the outcome of a psycho-spiritual crisis in the personality. Let me explain why. St Paul writes: 'Do not model yourselves on the behaviour of the world around you, but let your behaviour change, moulded by your new mind' (*Rom 12:2*). Plaster models are made in rubber moulds. As a result they assume the shape of the mould. Unconsciously our sense of self and values can be moulded by the world rather than by the Lord and his values. The secular self has a number of characteristics. Its sense of worth is secretly dependent on such things as success, reputation and status. It has a compulsive desire to acquire and defend these things, and a lurking fear of losing them. It tends to reject any experience from the outer or inner world that might threaten its sense of security and control.

During the kind of transitional crises we have already mentioned, the things that have been supporting the secular self are removed. Instead of enjoying success, status and a good reputation, a person may have to drink the bitter wine of failure, loss and humiliation. The embattled victim will put up stiff resistance to this process. That can explain why he worked frantically to retain the very things his secular self needs for a sense of well-being. As he loses the struggle, the sufferer is filled with fear, anger, hurt, etc. Often these feelings are repressed in a way that creates a lot of tension and strain. As this dynamic predominates, the secular self begins to run out of energy. It begins to suffer from a deep-seated exhaustion or 'burn-out'. The joy and peace of the past give way to spiritual desolation. Feelings of restlessness, agitation, hopelessness and sadness take hold. The Lord seems distant and unreal. Prayer is often abandoned or becomes formal. The person goes through the motions, but his heart is no longer in it. Spiritual things hold little or no attraction, while the things of the world and the flesh seem very attractive. Temptation is strong and weakness common. When it hits rock bottom, the personality can hit the 'Rock of Ages'. This happens in two stages. First, the person feels a heartfelt desire for a new experience of God. Second, the Lord answers this desire by revealing his love. This can have the effect of re-focusing the personality. It begins to move away from false, worldly values, to become more centred on Christ and his gospel. In this way St Paul's advice is fulfilled: 'You must give up your old way of life. You must put aside your old self, which gets corrupted by following illusory desires'. (It is this old self that suffers from stress and 'burn-out'). Your mind must be renewed by a spiritual revolution so that you can put on the new self that has been created in God's way. I should point out in passing that stress and desolation of spirit are not necessarily synonymous. Many people turn to the Lord with renewed energy during times of strain seeking his help. In cases like this stress can be seen as a providential opportunity of developing an even deeper relationship with the Lord.

OVERCOMING STRESS BY MEANS OF RELAXATION EXERCISES

Perhaps the most helpful thing a stressful person can do is to use a relaxation exercise. There are many of them, e.g. yoga, reflexology, imagery training, etc. We will look at three examples that I have found helpful — Benson's Relaxation Response, Schultz's Autogenic Training and Sanford's Serenity Exercise.

a) The Relaxation Response

Dr Herbert Benson was a professor of medicine at Harvard Medical School. His main interest was in high blood-pressure, which is often stress-related. He heard that experts in Transcendental Meditation had claimed that they could influence their autonomic functions such as heart rate and blood pressure. Benson thought that this was highly unlikely because the autonomic system is self governing and, by all accounts, beyond influence of mind or will. However, he invited some of these experts in TM to participate in clinical trials which could put their claims to the test. In the event, he was surprised to find that they could indeed lower their blood-pressure without the use of drugs.

Benson analysed the TM technique. Having stripped it of its Hindu content he found he could produce a secular version. It all depended on concentration. During times of stress the mind flits restlessly from one thing to another. It cannot focus on any single item for long. So TM tries to bring about tranquillity by encouraging meditation in a concentrated way on a meaningless word or mantra.

Benson wondered if it would not be better to use a word or phrase that would express the person's faith. He had a medical motive for this, based on the 'placebo effect'. Simply stated it refers to bodily changes produced by beliefs and expectations. As Benson writes: 'We know that *any* treatment is more likely to be successful if the patient has a great deal of faith in his physician's ability — or even faith that a higher spiritual power is at work in the body'. As a Christian I believe that there is such a higher power at work within the human body; we call it the Holy Spirit. Further I am convinced that when a person receives the Spirit in baptism, he also receives the peace and harmony of God. As a result I am sure that this peace is within us at all times, even when we are experiencing stress. It is like a treasure buried in the field of the heart. Therefore I can say without hesitation: '*The peace I want is within*'. This phrase expresses my faith.

Now Benson says that the faith effect is mobilised by using such a phrase as part of the secularised T.M. technique. Together they form the Relaxation Response, which can be outlined as follows:

1.   Sit in a comfortable position.

11

2.   Close your eyes, smile inwardly and relax your muscles.

3.   Focus on your breathing. Breathe slowly and naturally.

4.   Select a word or phrase that expresses your faith conviction e.g. 'maranatha' (which in Aramaic means 'come Lord Jesus') or 'the peace I want is within' (this is the ideal length for a mantra because it is seven syllables long). This word or phrase is repeated slowly on each outward breath. The key to the exercise is to try to think of nothing other than the words you are saying to yourself. In this connection Benson quotes the *Catholic Encyclopaedia* with approval when it says 'Attention is the very essence of prayer; as soon as this attention ceases, prayer ceases'.

5.   When distracting thoughts intrude and upset your attention, disregard them gently by saying something like 'Oh well'. Then quietly return to the word or phrase you are using. It is essential to maintain a passive relaxed attitude in dealing with any interruptions. Do not try to force yourself to attend. This will only make you tense and anxious about not succeeding.

If this exercise is followed for twenty minutes a day two things will happen. First, you will get used to using it. Second, it will have a very calming effect.

b)   Autogenic Training

Dr Johannes Schultz pioneered autogenic training as a means of relaxation in the 1920s. Over the years it has been perfected by other researchers, notably Dr Wolfgang Luthe. This method uses verbal cues to influence the autonomic system in order to produce deep relaxation. It is similar in many ways to the Relaxation Response in which one focuses attention on a word or phrase, while autogenic training focuses attention on physical sensations. So the key to this form of exercise is a sort of auto-suggestion called *Passive Concentration* which affirms that the body is getting heavy and warm. I often use it.

First, I try to become aware of the sensations in my feet,

noticing whether they are warm or cold, tense or relaxed. Then I imagine that they are getting heavy and warm. After a while I usually begin to sense the warmth. I focus my attention on that sensation and affirm that it is getting stronger. This is not done by a determined act of will. On the contrary it is a matter of believing that the gift of warmth is there to be discovered, so to speak. Having spent some time on my feet I might move to my hands and arms in a similar way. As I go through the exercise I can sense the tension leaving my muscles and a lovely feeling of relaxation spreading through my body. Here is a brief outline of the method.

1. Deep breathing exercises
   a) Imagine ocean waves rolling in . . . and out.
   b) Silently say to yourself: 'My breathing is smooth and rhythmic'.

2. Heartbeat regulation exercises
   a) Imagine ocean waves.
   b) Silently say: 'My heartbeat is slow and regular'.

3. Blood flow
   a) Right arm and hand
   — Silently say: 'My right arm and hand are heavy and warm'.
   — Imagine the warm sun shining on them.
   b) Left arm and hand
   — Silently say: 'My left arm and hand are heavy and warm'.
   — Imagine the warm sun shining on them.
   c) Legs and feet
   — Silently say: 'My legs and feet are heavy and warm'.
   — Imagine the warmth flowing down from the arms into the hands.

4. Summing up phrase
   'I am calm'.

5. Return to activity
   Move again from step one to step three.

c) A Serenity Exercise

Mrs Agnes Sanford was one of the pioneers in the rediscovery of the ministry of healing. In 1949 she published a book which has since become a classic. In it she describes a prayer exercise that I have adapted slightly.

1. Lay aside your cares and worries as best you can. Quieten your mind and concentrate on the reality of God. You may not know the Lord in a personal way. But you know that something sustains the universe. That something is not ourselves. So the first step is to remind yourself that there is a source of life outside yourself.

2. The second step is to get in touch with the source of life by saying a prayer like this: 'Heavenly Father, please increase in me at this time your life-giving power'. If you do not know this outside life as your Heavenly Father, you could simply say: 'Whoever you are — whatever you are — come into me now'.

3. The third step is to *believe* and *affirm* that the power is coming into you. Recall what Jesus promised: 'Whatever you ask for in prayer, believing you have it already, it will be yours' (*Mk 11:24*). Accept the power in faith. No matter how much you ask for something, it only becomes yours as you *accept it* and give thanks for it. 'Thank you', you can say, 'that your life is *now* coming into me and increasing life in my body, mind and spirit'.

4. The fourth step is to *observe* the operations of that life. In order to do this, you must decide on some tangible thing that you wish to be accomplished by that power, e.g. a decrease in stress and an increase of inner peace. You could say something like this: 'I thank you Lord, that the relaxation and peace I desire is being revealed within me, by the light of your Spirit'.

As we come to the end of this section, a final recommendation. Nowadays you can buy relaxation tapes in many shops. As you play them on a tape recorder you follow

14

the instructions of the speaker. A man who uses one, last thing at night, told me that he never heard the end of it, because he always fell asleep first. Listening to certain types of music can also be relaxing. There are many studies demonstrating the relaxing physiological responses to music, including changes in breathing, heart-rate, blood-pressure, blood supply, and galvanic skin responses. Some of the music of J. S. Bach is ideal for the purpose, e.g. his Concerto for Two Violins, his Harpsicord Concerto in F Minor for Flute and Strings and, finally, his Solo Harpsicord Concertos in F Major and C Major. The bigger record stores also sell what is called 'New Age Music' which is very relaxing.

OVERCOMING STRESS BY MEANS OF CHANGES IN LIFE-STYLE

In 1943 Reinhold Niebuhr wrote the following prayer: 'God give us the grace to accept with serenity the things that cannot be changed, courage to change the things which should be changed, and the wisdom to distinguish the one from the other'. The experience of chronic stress is an invitation to change the aspects of our lifestyle that contribute to it. They can and should be changed.

a) Establish priorities

It is important to discriminate between *needs* and *priorities*. Otherwise you will be swamped by an endless succession of urgent needs. A few years ago I had a chat with Sean, a curate in a Dublin parish. 'What are your priorities from a personal point of view?' I asked. 'I must admit,' he replied, 'that I haven't given the thing much thought'. 'As you think about it now', I said, 'what would you like your top priority to be?' Sean reflected for a while, then he said: 'I think that parish visitation should be my number one priority'. 'Well, do you get much time to visit?' I asked. 'Frankly, no', Sean replied, 'other things seem to demand my attention. For example, last night I had to attend a committee meeting. Tonight I'm judging a beauty competition in a local hotel, It's like that all the time'.

'But if pastoral visitation is a priority', I retorted, 'wouldn't it be better to say "no" to the many invitations you receive. You would feel that you were doing something really worthwhile, instead of feeling guilty about not visiting'.

That curate was no different from countless other people. Because he had failed to discriminate between needs and priorities he was hassled in a stressful way by countless demands on his time.

We begin to take control of our lives when we begin to establish long and short term goals, i.e. for the following year and the following day. Having made a list of between five and ten long-term goals, try to number them in their order of importance, 1, 2, 3, etc. Then try to work out a practical plan which indicates what has to be done and when. It is much the same when it comes to short-term goals for the following day. I read an interesting story in this connection. The president of an American steel company went to a New York consultant. 'I'll pay you any price,' he said, 'if you will tell me how to get more things done without undue stress.' The consultant replied: 'At night spend five minutes analysing your problems of the following day. Write them down on a sheet of paper, but place them in their order of importance. Then tackle the first item as soon as you get to the office. Stick to it until it is finished. Then move to the number two and so on. Test this method as long as you like, and then send me what you think it is worth.' Some time later the consultant received a note from the company president. Enclosed was a cheque for $25,000 with the words, 'For the most helpful advice I ever received.'

Evidently the New York consultant knew about the Pareto Principle, or the 80/20 rule. It states that if a person has listed ten goals in their order of importance, and tackles the top two, eighty per cent of his potential effectiveness will be derived from them. Only twenty per cent of his effectiveness will be derived from the other eight! People who fail to discriminate between top priorities and lesser ones, can end up using a lot of energy achieving very little. So time management is really worthwhile. It increases efficiency, while protecting the person from the tyranny of having to respond to endless needs. In the name of worthwhile priorities we can say 'no' with a good conscience. Instead of life controlling us, we can learn to regain control of our lives. As we do so, our stress levels will fall.

b) Exercise and diet

When we looked at chronic stress we saw that feelings of distress are due to the fact that our bodies are reacting to excessive levels of adrenalin and other substances. What is needed is some way of reducing those levels. Our ancestors would have done this by means of vigorous 'flight or fight'. We can have the same effect by taking exercise. It helps us to use up our surplus energy so that we feel more relaxed afterwards. Not only that, exercise helps us to become fit and contributes to our sense of well-being. There is also evidence to show that exercise enables the body to secrete chemicals that help to produce a state of physical harmony. Knowing this to be true one American professor of psychology refuses to see stressful or depressed clients unless they are willing to take an hour's walk every day. So why not plan to take some form of regular exercise such as swimming, jogging, golf, etc. It is important that you enjoy the exercise and that you set realistic goals for yourself. Otherwise you will not keep it up. For example, walking is an excellent form of exercise. You could plan to take a half-hour walk five days a week. It needs to be energetic enough to stimulate the heart to greater efforts.

Besides taking exercise, diet too can help to control tension. First, it is important to avoid taking chemicals that increase stress, e.g. caffeine, tannin, salt, nicotine, sugar and the like. In many cases substitutes like decaffeinated coffee and artificial sugars can be used. Where this is not possible moderation is the key to success. If you are over-weight try to plan a sensible diet. In other words, do it slowly. As you lose surplus pounds in this way, you will feel better physically and emotionally. Your stress levels will go down, while your self-esteem will go up.

c) The importance of leisure

People suffering from stress often complain about all the work they *have* to do. Yet when they could take time off, they avoid doing so because they would be unable to relax and face themselves. As a result they tend to take on more work, thereby reinforcing their stress. The only way to break out of this vicious circle is to *decide* to take time off for recreation. This can be done in three ways, in personal reflection, sharing with friends, and pursuing hobbies.

It is refreshing to spend time with oneself becoming aware of what is going on within. St Augustine wrote in his *Confessions*: 'Men go abroad to admire the heights and mountains, the mighty billows of the sea, the long courses of rivers, the vast extent of the ocean, the circular motion of the stars, and yet pass themselves by'.

There is a story in the life of Dr Carl Jung which illustrates the importance of this kind of self-intimacy. Apparently a society lady phoned him, to request an urgent appointment at 3 p.m. the following Thursday. Jung said it would not be possible because he already had an important appointment at that very time. Well, on the Thursday the same lady happened to sail past Jung's garden which ran down to the shores of Lake Zurich. There was the famous doctor, his shoes off, sitting on a wall, his feet dangling in the water. As soon as she got home the irate woman rang Jung demanding an explanation. 'You told me', she exclaimed, 'that you couldn't see me because you had an important appointment. Nevertheless I saw you at that very hour, whiling away the time at the bottom of your garden'. 'I told you no lie', the doctor replied, 'I had an appointment at that time, the most important of the week, *an appointment with myself.*'

The purpose of time on one's own is fourfold. First, I listen to my own experience in order to *recover* my feelings which can often lurk unrecognised in the twilight zone of preconsciousness. Second, I try to *name* my feelings. Instead of saying 'I feel good or bad about the invitation to the wedding', I try to be more specific about what I feel, e.g. 'I feel delighted', or 'surprised' or 'scared' by the invitation. It is good also to see where those feelings are coming from. As John Powell once wrote: 'Other people can stimulate my emotions, but the *causes* lie within'. Our affective reactions are rooted in our past experiences, e.g. I am threatened and scared by the wedding invitation because I am not good at handling social occasions, especially when the people present are better educated and more sophisticated. I always feel stupid and inferior at times like that just as I used to do when as a teenager I would ask a girl to dance. Third, I try to *own* my feelings, rather than thinking about them, or analysing them in a detached, dispassionate way. For example it would mean that instead of saying with a smile, 'I seem to have a lot of anger within me' I would say with a frown 'I am very angry, because I feel hurt and humiliated'. Fourth, it is good to *express* one's feelings, to a friend in conversation, and to God in prayer. Once I become aware of what is going on within me, and why, all sorts of issues can be faced and sorted out in a way that reduces stress.

Spending time with friends is also important. Our work then requires us to fulfil all kinds of roles and to keep our thoughts and feelings to ourselves, especially when they are negative ones. It is great when we can share them with someone who is prepared to listen with empathy and understanding. We can let off steam with friends in the knowledge that they will accept and love us as we are, and not as we pretend to be. This kind of mutual communication can have a very soothing, therapeutic effect, especially for natural extroverts. Often they only discover what they are thinking and feeling as they talk. Otherwise they become frustrated, lonely and stressful. As Bacon once said: 'The man or woman without friends becomes the cannibal of his own heart'. For more on this point see my *Christian Friendship*, published by All Hallows.

The pursuit of a hobby, such as music-making, painting, bird-watching, stamp-collecting, fishing, embroidery, wood-work, etc. can be relaxing and enjoyable. It is important to plan for leisure time. Unless this is a personal priority, it will be sacrificed in order to respond to all kinds of needs. The Comte de Mirabeau had the right idea when he wrote: 'I would not exchange my leisure hours for all the wealth in the world'. In my experience many people feel guilty about 'wasting time' on hobbies. Perhaps this reaction is rooted in the unconscious assumption of the work ethic, that a person is only lovable for what he does and not for who he is.

OVERCOMING STRESS BY CHANGING ATTITUDES

Earlier in this booklet it was stated that stress depends on a person's reactions, and not on outside events, e.g. having to talk in public could cause great stress in one person and none in another. The reason for the difference is psychological. Our reactions are rooted in our attitudes and beliefs, many of which can be unrealistic and unreasonable. In this section we are going to look at three such examples.

a) Irrational beliefs

A well known psychologist called Ellis has suggested that our feelings about events are predetermined by our beliefs and perceptions. As a result he talks about the ABC of emotions. It can be outlined as follows:

1. **A** refers to the Activating event, e.g. being licked on the face by a big dog.

2. **B** refers to Beliefs about the events, for example:
    — 'The dog likes me'
    — 'Dogs can bite you for no apparent reason'
    — 'Dogs are lovely cuddly creatures'
    — 'Dogs are man's best friends, loyal and true'.

    Clearly, these kinds of beliefs are often rooted in a person's life experience. One person may have been bitten by a dog in childhood, while another may have happy memories of a family pet.

3. **C** refers to Consequent feelings, ones that follow from one's belief about the event. For example, the person who believes that dogs are unhygienic or liable to attack, is going to feel fear, while the person who thinks that they are cuddly and loyal, is going to feel attraction and love.

Ellis maintained that a lot of stressful negative feelings are due to the fact that our beliefs about reality are both unrealistic and unreasonable. He thought that stress could be reduced if and when such irrational beliefs were recognised and changed. He and his followers have listed many of the common ones.

I will mention nine of them. See if any apply to you. Ask a friend what he or she thinks about your answers.

1. I need everyone's love and approval for about everything I do.'

2. I should be able to do everything well.

3. If something bad could, or does happen, I should worry about it.

4. It is easier to avoid difficult tasks, than to try them and risk failure.

5. I will enjoy life if I avoid responsibilities and take what I get right now.

6. A person's worth is directly related to his objectively discernible productivity.

7. Anger is automatically bad and destructive, and should always be repressed.

8. People are very fragile and one should keep one's thoughts to oneself in order to avoid hurting others.

9. Happiness, pleasure, fulfilment and growth can only be achieved in the company of others, never on one's own.

b) Coping with conflict in a constructive way

In relationships at home and at work, conflicts are inevitable. Here is a list of typical ones:

—   Having to say 'no' to a request for help.
—   Coping with criticism from another person, e.g. the boss.
—   Stating your rights and needs, e.g. in a restaurant.
—   Expressing negative feelings such as anger.
—   Giving a negative response to someone, having to confront them, e.g. telling a son or daughter they have to be home at midnight, not 3 in the morning.
—   Differing from the majority opinion at a meeting.
—   Making requests, e.g. asking a friend for money.
—   Initiating social contacts, e.g. at a wedding where you know none of the guests.

There are two stressful and inappropriate ways of coping with conflict. The first, is to be *passive*, to back down because of lack of self-esteem and the consequent belief that one should work for peace at any price. For example, one has arranged to meet a friend at 3 p.m. at the GPO in Dublin. She does not turn up until 3.30 and offers no explanation. You feel hurt and angry, but you smile and say nothing. To bury anger like this causes frustration and stress.

The second way of coping with a conflict situation is to become *aggressive* and overbearing. So when the friend turns up late, you attack her verbally: 'You are completely unreliable, your word means nothing. You don't give a damn about anybody'. Granted, this is a way of letting off emotional steam. But it is hurtful and will cause a rift between the two people and may evoke a counter-attack perhaps. Either way it will increase stress.

The third way of coping is to act *assertively*. When the friend arrives late I express what I feel: 'I felt hurt and angry when you didn't turn up at the time we arranged. I felt let-down and taken for granted'. In this way one lets off steam, but without attacking the other person and so stress levels can be reduced. This assertiveness can be used in all kinds of situations. For example, you are making a point at a meeting, when someone rudely interrupts. You can respond in a positive way by saying: 'Could you wait a moment, I want to finish my point, it is important to me'. This is better than going silent, or becoming aggressive. The same approach can be used in a shop where you were sold a defective article. 'The clock you sold me doesn't work correctly. I want a replacement'. If the assistant begins to argue the point, do not get involved, keep on asserting your position: 'The clock doesn't work. I want a new one please!' Many people find it hard to be assertive because of a lack of self-acceptance. If you wish to improve your self-acceptance. If you wish to improve your self-image see my *Self-esteem and the love of God* published by Veritas.

c) From obligation to personal conviction

Many people suffer from what has been called 'hardening of the oughteries'. They are normally motivated by a sense of cheerless obligation, the 'oughts, musts, and have-tos' of other people. As a result they begin to lose touch with their own deeper desires and inner freedom. Consequently, they may feel that they are losing control of their lives, and are hapless pawns on the chessboard of life. They spend their lives trying to please other people, not out of love, but because of fear, fear of condemnation or criticism. Needless to say this is a stressful experience. The way to overcome this sense of suffocation is to get used to asking the question, 'In the light of my beliefs and values, what do I *want* in these circumstances?' On getting in touch with what is going on within he will be in contact with his deepest self and his own freedom. As a result he will have an increased sense of autonomy and self-determination. He may do many of the same things as before, but for a different motive now.

BIBLICAL FAITH AND STRESS

The pace and pressures of modern life can be hectic. Crises of all kinds are common. If we learn to cope in the light of God's providence, we will cope much better. It is simply a matter of *nestling* in the Lord, rather than *wrestling* alone with difficulties. This point of view is illustrated over and over again in the Scriptures. We will examine one example from 2 Chronicles 20 in some detail.

a) Facing impossible odds

The Jewish King Jehoshaphat received news that his kingdom was about to be attacked by a huge army. From a military point of view the position was hopeless. Not surprisingly, the king was filled with fear and disquiet. But instead of magnifying the problem by focusing his attention on it, he magnified the Lord by focusing on him by means of prayer and fasting.

b) Hearing God's word and comfort

Having poured out his heart to the Lord, Jehoshaphat waited for his response. It came through one of his priests. Inspired by the Spirit he said: 'Your majesty, and all you people of

Judah and Jerusalem, the Lord says you must not be discouraged or afraid to face this large army. *The battle depends on God and not on you*'. This prophetic word finds an echo many times in the Scriptures.

— In Exodus 14:14 Moses says: 'Do not be afraid. Stand firm and you will see the deliverance the Lord will bring you today. *The Lord will fight for you, you need only be still*'.

— Normally we translate Psalm 37:7 as 'Be still and know that I am God'. However it could be more accurately translated as '*Stop fighting*, and know that I am God, supreme among the nations'.

In other words, when faced with difficulties, trust the Lord, do what he says and see what he will do on your behalf.

c) Anticipating victory in praise

Knowing that God would be true to his word, King Jehoshaphat worshipped the Lord while his priests praised him with loud voices. The following morning the king 'appointed men to sing to the Lord and to praise him for the splendour of his holiness as they went out at the head of the army'. This is a typical example of what is known in Hebrew as the 'teruwah Yahweh' or victory shout. It was a religious war cry meant to strike terror into enemies and to anticipate the manifestation of God's saving help. For example the 'victory shout' preceded the fall of Jericho. Again on Palm Sunday it anticipated the resurrection of Jesus and his victory over sin, Satan and death. Well, the king and his people believed in the Lord, and as a result they came to see the victory that they had desired, and which God had promised. Their enemies were defeated. The Jews had not to strike a blow!

THE WAY OF EXPRESSING FAITH IN TIMES OF STRESS

Having reflected on the biblical pattern of faith, we can go on to apply it in our own lives. There are three steps which spell the word THE.

- **T** refers to Thanking God no matter what happens.
- **H** refers to Handing our difficulties to the Lord.
- **E** refers to Expecting the Lord to help you.

Let us look at each step in turn.

a) Thanking God in all circumstances

On a number of occasions in the New Testament we are told:

- 'Pray constantly and for *all things* give thanks to the Lord' (*1 Thess 5:18*).
- '*Always* give thanks for *everything*, to God the Father' (*Eph 5:19*).
- 'If there is anything you need, pray for it, asking God for it with prayer and *thanksgiving*' (*Phil 4:6-7*).

So no matter what pressures and demands we have to face, we should pray with praise and thanksgiving. We do so in the belief that God will bring good out of the negative circumstances of our lives. The notion of the 'happy fault' lies behind this confidence in God's providence. It comes from the Easter liturgy, where the sin of Adam and Eve is referred to as a 'happy fault... which gained for us so great a Redeemer!' St Paul echoed this insight when he wrote that by turning *everything* to their good, God co-operates with those who love him (Rom 8:28). Having poured out one's feelings of distress to the Lord one goes on to express one's faith conviction to him in the form of praise and thanksgiving. In doing so many of us have found that it opens the heart to the graces God wants to give.

b) Handing our difficulties to the Lord

In 1 Peter 5:7 we read: 'Cast your anxieties on the Lord, for he cares about you'. Anxieties seems to have a gravitational pull that draws our attention away from God to ourselves. As a result many of us seem to cling to our worries and cares. It takes an act of will to reverse this dynamic. We have to make a *conscious decision* to hand over our lives and our problems into the care of God as we understand him.

c) Expect the Lord to help you

When we trust the Lord we can be sure that he will comfort us. As St Paul says: 'God helps us in all our troubles' (*2 Cor 1:4-5*). No matter how weak and vulnerable we may feel, 'God's power is made perfect in our weakness' (*2 Cor 12:8*). I had a memorable experience of this truth a couple of years ago. I had been invited to speak at a conference, for Italians only, in Assisi. When I got to Rome en route to my destination, I was suffering from chronic stress. I was anxious about everything. What would I say at the conference? Would my interpreter be able to cope? Would I be able to find out what buses and trains I would need to get to my engagement? The more I thought about these things, the more my stress increased. I had a blinding headache. My body was like a wound-up spring. Finally, I turned to the Lord. I poured out my feelings, all of them negative, having tried to thank the Lord, I implored him to help me. After a while I recalled a text in Isaiah 41:10 'Fear not, I am with you, be not dismayed, for I am your God, I will strengthen you, I will uphold you with my victorious right hand'. 'I will strengthen and uphold you'. That was just what I needed to hear. I asked the Lord to carry out his promises. Nothing seemed to happen. I felt very disappointed, and told the Lord so. Then I went back to the verse and noticed that the Lord had said: 'Fear not, be not dismayed'. Perhaps this was not a word of advice, but rather a command. So I said to the Lord: 'Be it done unto me according to thy word. If you want me to be courageous I *will* be courageous. I'll take on the whole of Italy if necessary. But you must help me'. Well, it was like a miracle. As soon as I said this prayer a cloud of peace came upon me. My headache disappeared. My tension melted. Stress was replaced by a quiet confidence in the Lord. It never deserted me. I sailed through the conference without a worry. The Lord had been as good as his word.

CONCLUSION
Over a period of time I have come to appreciate the fact that there is a difference between physical relaxation and spiritual

peace. Needless to say there is a connection between the two. But it is quite possible to imagine that a person would be suffering from stress while being at peace deep down in his heart, on account of having a good conscience and confidence in God's loving mercy. It is also possible to imagine that a person could be physically relaxed while being spiritually agitated and desolate for one reason or another.

During a recent visit to Medjugorje I was impressed by the messages that seem to come from Our Lady, Queen of Peace. I want to end this booklet with two of them. The first is for our everyday lives: 'If you want to be very happy, live a simple, humble life, pray a lot, and don't worry and fret over your problems — let them be settled by God'. The second message concerns the future: 'Don't think about wars, chastisements, evil. It is when you concentrate on these things that you are on the way to enter into them. Your responsibility is to accept divine peace, live it'.

SCRIPTURE TEXTS FOR TIMES OF STRESS

The following scripture texts may provide you with guidance and strength in times of stress:

1. *Joshua* 1:9
    'Remember that I have commanded you to be determined and confident! Don't be afraid or discouraged, for I, the Lord your God, am with you wherever you go.'

2. *Isaiah* 41:10
    'Fear not, for I am with you, be not dismayed, for I am your God; I will strengthen you, I will uphold you with my victorious right hand.'

3. *2 Chronicles* 20:15
    'The Lord says that you must not be discouraged or be afraid... the battle depends on God, not on you.'

4. *Exodus* 14:13
    'Do not be afraid! Stand by and see the salvation of the

Lord which he will accomplish for you today... The Lord will fight for you while you keep silent.'

5. *Jeremiah* 17:7-9
    'But I will bless the person who puts his trust in me. He is like a tree growing near a stream and sending out roots to the water. It is not afraid when hot weather comes, because its leaves stay green; it has no worries when there is no rain; it keeps on bearing fruit.'

6. 2 *Chronicles* 14:11
    'Yahweh, no one but you can stand up for the powerless against the powerful. Come to our help. Yahweh our God! We rely on you, and confront this crisis in your name. Yahweh, you are our God. Let man leave everything to you.'

7. *Daniel* 10:17-20
    'For now I have no strength, and no breath is left in me. Again one having the appearance of a man touched me and strengthened me. And he said: "Oh, man greatly beloved, fear not, peace be with you; be strong and of good courage".'

8. *John* 16:13
    'You will have peace by being united to me. The world will make you suffer. But be brave! I have overcome the world.'

9. *Romans* 8:31
    'If God is for us, who is against us?'

10. *Hebrews* 13:5-7
    'The Lord has said: "I will never fail you nor forsake you". Hence we confidently say: "The Lord is my helper, I will not be afraid; what can man do to me?" '

11. 1 *Peter* 5:7
    'Cast all your anxieties on the Lord because he cares about you.'

12. *Psalm* 34:18
'The Lord is near the brokenhearted, and saves the crushed in spirit.'

13. *Matthew* 11:29-30
'Come to me, all who labour and are heavily laden, and I will give you rest. Take my yoke upon you, and learn from me, for I am gentle and humble of heart, and you will find rest for your souls.'

> 'Let nothing perturb you,
> Nothing frighten you.
> All things pass.
> God does not change.
> Patience achieves everything.
> Whoever has God, lacks nothing.
> God alone suffices.'
>
> *St Teresa of Avila*